PERSONAL
PRODUCTIVITY

Henry E. Liebling

PRODUCTIVITY

Copyright © 1989 by Skill Builders, Inc.

Additional copies of this book are available from
the publisher. Address all inquiries to:

Productivity Press
P.O. Box 13390
Portland, OR   97213-0390
United States of America
Telephone: (503) 235-0600
Telefax: (503) 235-0909
E-mail: service@ppress.com

ISBN: 0-56327-131-1

Printed in the United States of America

01 00 99 98 97 96   12 11 10 9 8 7

CONTENTS

INDEX

INDEX

GETTING STARTED

Here are a few suggestions to consider when using PERSONAL PRODUCTIVITY.

1. **Choose which chapter or section matters the most**.

   Decide:
   - what you want to learn
   - what you want to improve
   - what you want to achieve

2. **Challenge yourself with a new vision**. Invest in yourself and watch yourself grow. Think of growth and change as an opportunity that will bring you many rewards.

3. **Make sure you follow-through with your ideas; this will improve your learning and effectiveness**. Practice the THINGS TO DO suggestions that you choose. Complete the exercises on separate sheets of paper. Take notes if you like. Integrate the material into <u>all</u> aspects of your life.

4. **Review your progress**. How are you doing? What are you doing differently today from what you did in the past? Are you still focusing on your new vision? Are you completing the things you need to accomplish in order to achieve your new vision?

5. **Handle set-backs as temporary and keep moving yourself toward your vision**. The most successful people and organizations in the world have set-backs. <u>Remember</u>: It's not what happens to you that matters; it is how you handle the situation that matters. Learn what you can about why the set-back occurred. Develop the habit of encouraging yourself.

6. **Motivation**. Your formula for success must include belief, determination, and effort.

   If necessary, get re-energized by reviewing the motivation for your goal. (See p. 29)

ABILITY

ABILITY ALONE IS NOT ENOUGH FOR SUCCESS.

IT MUST BE SPARKED BY AMBITION AND SUSTAINED BY INTEGRITY AND DETERMINATION.

MANY AN ABLE PERSON FAILS TO ACHIEVE ANYTHING WORTHWHILE BECAUSE HE OR SHE JUST DOES NOT CARE. MANY WHO DO CARE LOSE OUT BECAUSE THEY CANNOT BE TRUSTED, AND OTHERS WHO ARE ABLE, AMBITIOUS, AND TRUSTWORTHY SIMPLY GIVE UP TOO SOON.

IT IS ESSENTIAL THAT THE FOUR WORKHORSES OF SUCCESS.... ABILITY, AMBITION, INTEGRITY, AND DETERMINATION.... PULL TOGETHER AS A TEAM UNTIL THEIR WORK IS DONE.

Anonymous

PERSONAL
PRODUCTIVITY

SELF-ESTEEM

Self-esteem (self-respect, feeling of self-worth) is how you feel about yourself.

People with high self-esteem like themselves, feel warm and loving toward themselves, and have a positive opinion about who they are as a person.

The better you feel about yourself, the easier it is to impart feelings of respect and esteem to others (co-workers, customers/clients, family members, and friends).

THINGS TO DO

1. **Be encouraging to yourself**. Don't put yourself down. Think about your successes, however small. Don't dwell on things in the past that did not work out. Feel good about what you have achieved. Think about what is right with your life. Count your blessings.

2. **Build self-esteem through positive self-talk**. Repeating to yourself positive phrases is positive self-talk. This builds self-esteem. (See pages 14-16)

3. **Practice liking yourself**. Think about your personal qualities. Which ones do you feel good about? What are the things you do that make you feel good about yourself? Write these down and refer to this list often.

4. **Accept yourself as a unique and special person**. Listen to your feelings and observe yourself. Try to enjoy and appreciate who you are.

    If you see behavior or personality traits that you want to change, have confidence that you will change them. Feel good about wanting to grow.

5. **Hold onto your good feelings about yourself**. Do not let other people's negative or differing opinions lessen your respect for yourself.

6. **Compliment yourself**. After you do something correctly, feel good about it and say to yourself:

   I did a good job.

   I'm proud of myself.

   Darn, I'm good!

7. **Enjoy compliments from others**. Develop the habit of feeling good when you get a compliment. Acknowledge compliments with a "thank you."

   Be careful about depending on compliments as your only method for building your self-esteem.

Challenge Yourself Exercises

1. **Which self-esteem THINGS TO DO suggestions will you use more frequently?**

2. **Like yourself.** Make a list of at least ten things you like about yourself.

    When making your list, consider your personality traits and the things you enjoy doing.

    Periodically, review what you have written.

3. **Compliment yourself.** Can you think of any situations where you could have complimented yourself because you did something right?

AFFIRMATIONS

<u>Instructions</u>: To yourself, repeat (read, mentally picture, and vividly imagine) these positive affirmations until you develop the habit of thinking this way.

I like and appreciate myself.

I encourage myself and others.

I feel warm and loving toward myself.

*I am my own best friend and I
do at least one thing each day
to remind me of this wonderful fact.*

*I treat my co-workers and team
members with dignity and respect.*

I enjoy compliments and say "thank you."

*I "let go" of habits that are
no longer relevant to my goals.*

AFFIRMATIONS

I never devalue myself or others.

I am an action-person; I do first things first and one thing at a time.

I am actively in charge of my life and I direct it in constructive ways.

I expect to reach my goals and I bounce back from temporary setbacks.

I can learn this new material.

I can master this new procedure.

It's not what happens to me, but how I handle it that determines my emotional well-being.

I aim for excellence.

I am a well-organized person.

AFFIRMATIONS

*I am in total control to decide how much
time I set aside for physical exercise.*

*It's easy for me to say "no"
to extra helpings of food.*

*I am alert to new ideas and new
methods that I can use in my job.*

*Everyday is an opportunity to achieve, to
learn something new, to be the best I can
be, and to foster team spirit.*

I look for ways to help other people.

*I respect opinions that are different from my
own, and I work through whatever
disagreements that may arise.*

I eliminate recurring problems.

BAN NEGATIVE THINKING

Instructions: Avoid self-defeating thoughts that can lower your self-esteem and vision.

"I can't."

"We can't."

"It's never been done before, so it probably won't work."

"I'll never amount to anything."

"We'll never get out of this rut."

"I'll never be able to learn that."

"This new procedure is going to be impossible to implement."

"We'll never meet our deadline."

"I'm always late for meetings."

"I can't get myself organized."

BAN NEGATIVE THINKING

"That person (department) never understands what I have to say."

"I can never remember names."

"They won't like what I am selling."

"I'm not good at influencing others."

"There is never enough time. I always have work to take home with me."

"I always feel immobilized when I hear a customer's complaint."

"I always feel stressed out when things change around here."

"I always over-eat and eat too fast."

"I always get bogged down with trivia."

"I always make mistakes when I input data into the computer."

Challenge Yourself Exercises

4. **Positive Self-Talk Affirmations**. After reading the affirmations on pages 14 - 18, do you feel your "self-talk" (what you tell yourself in your mental conversation) is more "positive" or more "negative"?

5. **Become more positive**. List the positive affirmations you will use more frequently. What negative self-talk will you work to eliminate?

6. **Self-fulfilling prophecies**. Have you experienced any self-fulfilling prophecies? Were they good or bad for your life? (A self-fulfilling prophecy is something that you predict will happen and it usually does.)

7. **The Building Self-Esteem Game**. Challenge yourself, and others, to see how long you can go without putting yourself and others down.

SETTING GOALS

A goal is something you strive to attain. It is an aim, a purpose, a target, a mission, an ambition or an objective. Goals provide you purpose and direction.

THINGS TO DO

1. **Set goals in many areas of your life so that you have balanced direction**.

   . self-esteem
   . physical health
   . mental health
   . family
   . recreation
   . hobbies
   . politics
   . financial
   . social
   . eating habits
   . personal habits

   . career/job
   . volunteering
   . religious/spiritual
   . education
   . retirement
   . friendships
   . travel
   . leisure/relaxation
   . others _____

Challenge Yourself Exercises

8. **Referring to page 20, what areas are most important to you?**

   First _____

   Second _____

   Third _____

   Fourth _____

   Fifth _____

2. **Make your goals specific (clarity).**
   Define your goals so you can measure
   them in time, quantity, and quality.
   (See p. 22) This will enable you to:

   - develop a plan of action
   - budget your time
   - involve others
   - measure your progress
   - appreciate your progress

EXAMPLES OF QUESTIONS TO HELP
MAKE GOALS MORE SPECIFIC

I want to be more effective.
  *Specifically, what does "more effective"
  mean to you?*

I want to do a better job.
  What does "better job" mean to you?

I want to use my time better.
  What does "better" mean to you?

I'm going to start exercising.
  *On what day will you start? How many
  days each week? How many minutes
  each session? What type of exercise
  works best for you?*

I want to lose weight.
  What is the weight you are aiming for?

I'm going to return my telephone calls faster.
  *What percentage (50, 75, 100%) of your
  calls will you return within 4-hours?
  within 24-hours?*

Challenge Yourself Exercises

9. **What are your goals?** In Exercise No.
   8, you were asked to list your five most
   important areas in your life.

   Now, write at least three or four
   sentences or phrases that describes
   your goal for each of these areas.
   Elaborate on each one and be as
   specific as possible. Use a separate
   sheet of paper for each goal you are
   describing.

10. **Improvement goals**. If you were to
    make improvements in your life, what
    improvements would you make? (at
    work? at home?) Be as specific as
    possible.

Remember: **Write your goals down.**

3. **Make sure your goals are positive**.
   Focus on what you want.
   (Read left to right)

Positive Goal	Negative Goal
I expect to be on time. I arrive 15 minutes ahead of schedule.	"I don't want to be late."
I intend to make this sale.	"I don't want to lose this sale."
I intend to listen carefully.	"I don't want to be an insensitive listener."
I eat what I plan.	"I don't want to overeat."
We expect to be successful.	"We don't want to fail."

Challenge Yourself Exercises

11. How would you convert the following "negative" goals into "positive" statements?

We don't want to offend our customers.
Positive:_____

We don't want to let the phone ring over and over again.
Positive:_____

We don't want to rework this item a 2nd or 3rd time.
Positive:_____

I don't want to be inefficient.
Positive:_____

I don't want to flub up this interview.
Positive:_____

4. **Goals work together**. Try to have goals that are compatible with each other.

    Example: A parent sets several goals at the same time... (1) to increase family time together, (2) to participate in community affairs, and (3) to add a change of pace from paid-work.

    Action: The parent gets the family to participate together as volunteers with a local organization.

5. **Update or set new goals to regain drive, enthusiasm, and momentum.** If you feel that you are in a rut or have reached a plateau, you may have lost momentum. You can regain drive and enthusiasm by setting and visualizing new goals. (See p. 27)

Challenge Yourself Exercises

12. **Do you feel a need to update or modify any of your goals?**

Goal	Updated Goal
Get new customers.	Keep them satisfied.
Buy new equip-, ment, computer, software, or telephone system.	Install it properly. Train the people how to use it.
Complete the plan or budget.	Implement it.
Go to the training workshop.	Apply what you learn.
Get the new job or position.	Succeed at it.
Read this book.	Use what's in it.
Go on a vacation.	Have fun. Meet new people.

PLAN OF ACTION

A plan of action is a written guide that helps you focus your attention, organize your thoughts, and identify what you need to do to reach your goals.

Too often, plans are only thought about and not put into action. By committing your plans to paper and reviewing/updating them, they take on added meaning.

SEVEN STEPS

I. General goal

2. Motivation

3. Objectives

4. What needs to be accomplished?

5. Visualization

6. Contingencies and flexibility

7. Internalizing and reinforcing

Step 1   General Goal

Write out your goal in broad, general terms. **1**
What do you want to achieve?

Step 2   Motivation

List "why" you want, or choose, to reach this
goal. What will it bring you? What's in it for
you? How do you think you will feel when
the goal is achieved?

Step 3   Objectives

Break-down your general goal into smaller,
more manageable pieces (specific objectives,
sub-goals, "smaller goals"). Write your
specific objectives (sub-goals) on paper.

Suggestion: Give yourself credit for
accomplishing your sub-goals... but don't rest
on your laurels.

Step 4   What needs to be accomplished?

List what needs to be accomplished to reach your goal.

Step 5   Visualization

Visualize in your mind:

- your general goal
  (Step 1)

- your specific objective(s)
  (Step 3)

- the actions you will be taking
  (Step 4)

Imagine how good you will feel when your reach your goal.

Step 6   Contingencies and flexibility

Alternate actions may be necessary if
something goes wrong or if you run into a
road-block. Stay flexible. Be prepared.
Anticipate.

Contingency planning is identifying possible
problems before they occur and having
alternative actions already in mind should any
problems arise.

Step 7   Internalizing and reinforcing

Internalize your written plan by referring to it
often. This keeps you focused.

Other internalizing methods are:

(A)   Put your plan of action on audio tape
and listen to it repeatedly.

(B)   Transfer key parts of your plan to 3x5
index cards. Carry them with you and
refer to them frequently.

Challenge Yourself Exercises

13. **Workplace goal setting**. Choose a workplace goal. Ask yourself: How does this goal fit into your department's purpose?

    Now, write 5 - 10 sentences or phrases that describes this goal. Provide as much detail as you can.

14. **Personal goal setting**. Refer to your answers in Exercise No. 9.

    Select a goal you want to work on. Then, using an 8 1/2 x 11 sheet of paper, complete your Plan of Action for this goal, using the seven steps.

VISUALIZATION

Visualization (mental imagery, visioning) is a powerful technique for using the creative powers of your mind to help you achieve goals.

Develop a mental picture of your goal. See your goal as if you have already achieved it or as if you are in the process of achieving it.

The technique works best when you frequently repeat the visualization process over an extended period of time. Adding positive self-talk for additional reinforcement makes visualization more effective.

EXAMPLES

Sports. See in your mind's eye where you want the ball (arrow, horseshoe, or puck) to go.

Writing. Visualize yourself working on the report or paper. Imagine how you will feel when you see the project completed.

Customer service. Visualize yourself asking: "Is there any way that I can help you?" or "What else can I help you with?" or "Is everything okay?" Imagine the customer's satisfied reaction to your service.

Handling complaints. See yourself listening carefully and patiently to a customer venting his or her feelings. Visualize yourself handling the complaint politely, competently and efficiently.

Selling. See yourself... making a professional presentation; asking questions so that you understand needs; discussing or demonstrating the benefits; answering the buyer's questions in a confident and empathetic manner; asking for the order; and hearing the buyer say YES. See yourself providing follow-up service and support.

Eating habits. Visualize yourself saying "no" to extra helpings of food. See yourself eating at a proper pace and chewing your food. Visualize yourself eating food that is healthy for you and in appropriate amounts.

Learning to use equipment.   Visualize yourself in front of the equipment (computer, FAX, VCR, robot, telephone system, etc.). Visualize your precise physical relationship to the equipment, how you will stand or sit, and where your hands will go. See yourself using the equipment. See yourself flipping through the operator's manual to find an answer to a question. Imagine feeling confident about having mastered a new technique.

Energize yourself.   Visualize yourself at an event from your past (seminar, workshop, meeting, luncheon, dance) when you felt really terrific or had a powerful learning experience. Visualize the specific event that had caused the good feeling or experience.

Leadership.   See yourself as a leader ... sharing your ideas; listening to and working with others to solve or prevent problems; reminding people about goals and purpose; encouraging others; and having a positive attitude toward change.

Remember: **Anyone can be a leader!**

Tests.   Before the test, see yourself taking the test and feeling good about it. Imagine how you will feel upon successful completion.

Public speaking.   Visualize yourself being introduced; walking toward the stage; successfully walking up the steps; walking toward the podium; seeing faces in the audience; and being poised as you begin to speak. See the audience paying attention to you as you confidently and competently discuss your topic.

Nervousness.   Nervous about a party or new situation? Visualize yourself as confident and competent in a situation where you normally feel nervous. In your mental picture, note how you sound, behave, and positively influence others.

Challenge Yourself Exercises

15. **Practice visualization**.   List several situations in which you think you would personally benefit by practicing visualization.

TIME MANAGEMENT

Time management is self-leadership. Time exists; it is not something you can change. You can, however, lead your life so that you use time to your best advantage.

THINGS TO DO

1. **Focus your effort on what matters the most. Set priorities**. Decide what goals and what activities are most important. Focus on the essentials. Eliminate low priority items.

   Prepare a TO DO LIST for the following day. Rank your goals and activities in terms of URGENT, HIGH, MEDIUM and LOW. (See p. 40)

2. **Begin each day with a definite plan**. Refer to the TO DO LIST that you prepared the day before.

3. **On-going learning**. Train yourself to use new concepts, new tools, new procedures, and new technologies. Look for ways to streamline your work.

4. **Organization**. Develop systems so that you do not waste time shuffling paper-items (bills, memos, reports, magazines). Handle paper-items as few times as possible.

5. **Think of set-backs as temporary situations**.

6. **Be willing to change habits**. Get rid of habits that are not relevant to your goals.

   As you grow as a person, analyze your habits to make sure they support your goals.

7. **Do not worry about what did not get completed**. You can not fix something that is past.

8. **Clarity of direction**. Be clear about your standards, values, and principles. Use them as criteria in making decisions.

9. **Time out for renewal**. Allocate time to refresh yourself by relaxing and enjoying quiet time. Seek activities that bring you energy, enthusiasm, satisfaction, and balance.

10. **Invest your time to prevent problems**. It is not efficient to use your time for re-occurring problems. Invest your time to prevent problems.

11. **Get excited about your goals by visualizing them as already accomplished**. Imagine the good things that will result when your goals are achieved.

TO DO LIST

ACTIVITY/GOAL	PRIORITY			
	U	H	M	L

COMPLETE HIGH PRIORITY & URGENT ITEMS

Challenge Yourself Exercises

16. **Time management improvements**. Which time management THINGS TO DO suggestions will you use more frequently at work? at home?

17. **Habits**. Based on your current goals, which habits do you feel you need to change?

18. **New goals**. Do you have a new goal, a new job, or different needs that require new behavior, new habits and new ways of using time?

19. **Private time**. Using your personal appointments calendar, right now schedule a private time with yourself. Use this special time to work on things that will help you achieve your goals.

PERSONAL TIME INVENTORY

1. **Maintain an accurate log** of everything you do in one week's time. (Do this at least two times a year.)

   This honestly compiled inventory will provide a picture of how you use time and how much time you really control.

2. **Analyze your findings in relationship to your goals**. Discuss your findings with team members (co-workers, colleagues and family.)

3. **Use the information to make decisions about your self-leadership.**

   - Activities you need to **stop** (**change**) because they sabotage your progress.

   - Activities you need to **add** (**start**).

   - Activities you need to **continue** to do.

<u>Suggestion</u>: Right now, schedule into your calendar the two one-week periods.

SNATCHING TIME

The time you "save" each day adds up and can be redirected to new activities.

By "saving" just 30 minutes each day (or 60 minutes every other day), you will have 15 hours of new time each month. On a yearly basis, this is just like having an extra 180 hours (twenty-two 8-hour days).

Saved Time	New Time		
	each year	each month	each week
20 min. per day	120 hrs.	10 hrs.	2 hrs.
30 min. per day	180 hrs.	15 hrs.	3 hrs.
60 min. per day	365 hrs.	30 hrs.	6 hrs.

Challenge Yourself Exercises

20. **What can you change so that you snatch some time?**

21. **How might you use your new time?**

COMMUNICATIONS

Consistent use of the communication skills in this chapter will make your relationships work better for you, and will improve your effectiveness.

Communication occurs when the "receiving-person" understands what the "sending-person" is meaning.

Communication is a process. Remember: The feelings and prior experiences of the receiver and sender, plus the timing of the communication, affect this process.

THINGS TO DO

LISTENING SKILLS - THE RECEIVER

1. **Listen carefully and concentrate**.
    Listen with your eyes and ears. What do the <u>words</u> say? What does the <u>voice</u> and <u>body language</u> tell you?

Avoid mentally racing ahead or drifting to another topic. Try to identify the primary message that is being communicated.

2. **Ask questions and restate for clarity**. Strive for mutual understanding with the sender. Check your interpretation of what was said by repeating back to the sender what you heard. <u>Examples</u>:

   This is what I think you said (insert), am I on target?

   Would you say that again?

   I'm not sure I understand, would you say it in another way?

   I missed part of that, would you please repeat it?

3. **Do not interrupt**. Wait until the sender has finished his or her statement, or there is a natural pause, before you comment.

4. **Have an open mind about new ideas and information**. Just because the idea is new, or different from your point of view, is no reason to reject the new idea or the person who brought it to you. Work at understanding and respecting other points of view.

    If you do not welcome ideas, people will stop sharing them with you. If you put-down or are slow to respond to people who report problems, they will stop bringing this information to your attention.

SPEAKING SKILLS - THE SENDER

1. **Accept responsibility for making sure your message is understood**. Be imaginative in getting your point across. Remember: What you say may not be what is heard. Strive for mutual understanding with the receiver.

    Be sure to explain "why" when explaining policies or changes.

2. **Respect and understand the receiver.**
   Avoid jargon that the receiver is not
   familiar with. Try to see things from the
   receiver's point of view. Be patient with
   people who see things differently than
   you. Remember: The receiver's feelings
   will affect how your message is
   interpreted.

   Having respect for others doesn't mean
   anything unless you demonstrate it.
   Make sure you use examples, words,
   phrases, and images that will be
   understood.

3. **Sustain interest.** Direct your message
   so that these questions get answered:

   What benefit is this to me?

   What will this do for me?

   What's in it for me?

4. **Be as specific as possible**. Avoid vagueness. Don't assume people have the same understanding of certain words as you do. Work for mutual clarity with the receiver.

The following phrases usually need clarification:

Let's improve service.
The training will be participative.
I'll be home in a little while.
I'll be ready in a little while.

5. **Involve the receiver so you have a two-way process**. Avoid one-way messages whenever possible. Get feedback by asking the person to whom you are speaking to repeat back in his or her own words what you have said. This will help you know whether or not you are being understood.

Remember: A two-way process helps the people who are communicating with each other to feel they are talking "with" and not "at" each other.

EXAMPLES OF FEEDBACK QUESTIONS

1

What would you like to add?

Would you please repeat what I have just said?

What's your opinion?

What do you think?

Challenge Yourself Exercises

22. **Improving workplace relationships.** Make a list of several THINGS TO DO suggestions that would improve your workplace listening and communication skills.

23. **Improving personal relationships.** Make a list of several THINGS TO DO suggestions that would help you improve your personal relationships at home and with friends.

Letters and Memos

Customers (clients) judge you and your employer by the quality of the letters you send them. Strive to satisfy the need(s) of the person to whom you are writing. Write your letters so they properly represent yourself and your employer.

THINGS TO DO

1. As you prepare, ask yourself: **"What am I trying to accomplish?"**

2. Space your letter so that it **creates a favorable impression** on first sight. Use short paragraphs.

3. The letter that is **correct in spelling and grammar** shows your thoroughness and concern. Make use of desktop reference books and word processor spell-checkers to ensure quality.

* Contributed by Gold Consulting, New York City

4. Compose your letter so that it has a **positive tone**. Which is more positive to you, (A) or (B)?

    (A)   We can't send you the magazine until March 25.

    (B)   We can send you the magazine as early as March 25.

5. Give your letter a **friendly "sound."** Use words like *please* and *thank you.* Omit words like *should, must, have to,* and *the above mentioned.*

6. **Let your personality shine through** to your readers. Avoid *as per, pursuant to,* and *please find.*

7. Make any **requests clear and straightforward**. If you are not sure how your memo is coming across, ask a co-worker for feedback.

8. Is your letter **easy to read?** Simplify it by minimizing prepositions (*to, for, from, in, by*).

   Streamline: *Please let us hear from you as to your intentions concerning this matter.*

   To read: *Please tell us your plans.*

   or *Please tell us what you would like to do.*

9. To build your customer's confidence, be sure your letter **gives enough facts**. When you are answering a customer inquiry about a delivery, make sure your letter tells the arrival date of the package and method of shipping.

10. Focus on your reader's needs and build good-will by using **the "you" approach** in your writing.

    Successful people sprinkle their correspondence with the words *you* and *your*.

COACHING

Coaching is a person-to-person activity to help people develop their knowledge, mental attitude, and skills. The coach (manager, supervisor, teacher, parent) needs to emphasize a positive approach.

The person being coached needs to knows the difference between the right way and the wrong way of doing something, and understand "why" one method is preferred over another. Do not reinforce negative behavior by stressing what is not to be accomplished. Accent the positive.

(Read left to right)

Right Way	**Wrong Way**
Let me explain why I need the report by noon each Tuesday.	You always get your reports in late.
Keep your eye on the ball until it hits your mitt.	You always close your eyes before you catch the ball.

Right Way	**Wrong Way**
Answer the phone before the third ring.	You don't answer the phone fast enough.
Run every document through spell-check.	You never use the word processor spell-check.
Be prepared for the meeting and bring your notes.	You never come to meetings prepared.
It's important to leave yourself enough time so that your paper truly reflects your good ideas and best work.	You always wait till the last minute to do your term paper.

INFLUENCE & PERSUASION

1

Influencing and persuading another person means helping that person understand and appreciate how your idea (service, product, suggestion, proposal or innovation) satisfies their self-interest.

THINGS TO DO

1. **Be specific - know what you want**.
   What is your goal? What do you want to accomplish? If it's not crystal - clear to you, it will be confusing to others.

2. **Friendliness and sincerity**. Having these qualities will give you a foundation for getting what you want. They do not guarantee results, but without them you put yourself at a disadvantage.

3. **Benefits. What's in it for me?**
   This is the question the other party needs answered. Explain the benefits of your proposal from the point of view of the other person.

4. **Empathy and understanding**. Develop empathy for others: try to see things from their point of view. Focus your communication skills and explanations on the special needs of the person with whom you are communicating.

5. **Listen and learn**. Ask questions. Find out what the other person needs. Find out how you can provide service.

6. **Believe in yourself**. Believe in what you are trying to accomplish. The two P's of success are: persistence and patience.

7. **Rehearse**. Write out your presentation. Use the visualization technique - rehearse in your mind.

8. **Build your self-confidence by preparing yourself to answer questions**. Anticipate the questions you will probably hear.

9. **Follow-Up**. Set-up procedures and systems so you follow-through with whatever you agreed to do. This earns you trust and respect.

10. **Time**. Use your time so that you direct your efforts toward people who can make or influence decisions and help you get what you want.

    If you work as a salesperson, direct your efforts toward buyers.

11. **Continuous self-improvement**. Review your work habits and activities on a weekly basis. Look for ways to be more effective. Seek out people, books, and tapes that can help you grow.

12. **Networking and referrals**. Ask customers, clients, and friends for names of people who might help you. Meet new people at meetings and through volunteer work.

13. **Administrative procedures**. Learn how things are handled by the organization, or the individual, with whom you are dealing. This will give you an edge in getting information and paperwork through the organization.

14. **CLOSING**. Do you remember your goal? Work toward the other person (buyer) being in agreement with what you want to accomplish.

Challenge Yourself Exercises

24. **Things to work on**. If you were coaching yourself to be a superstar at influencing others, what THINGS TO DO suggestions would you work on?

25. **Sales effectiveness**. What THINGS TO DO suggestions will you work on?

26. **Leadership effectiveness**. As a manager or supervisor, which THINGS TO DO suggestions can you use to improve your effectiveness?

TEAM ACHIEVEMENT

TEAM ACHIEVEMENT

Teamwork (partnerships, collaboration) begins with a state of mind.

There needs to be a willingness to:
- *cooperate*
- *share*
- *trust*
- *listen*
- *give assistance & support to others*
- *accept help & support*
- *involve & accept new people*
- *exchange information*

Great things can happen when people work together as a team, especially among people representing different departments, professional disciplines, and backgrounds.

Teamwork needs to be practiced throughout our society... in our workplaces, educational institutions, government agencies, volunteer organizations, communities, and families.

THINGS TO DO

1. **Keep the big picture in mind**. Strive to help the organization-as-a-whole achieve its purpose (mission) so that its clients, customers, and staff are fully satisfied.

2. **Stimulate innovation through CROSS FUNCTIONAL (horizontal and "diagonal slice" across diverse grade levels) communication, cooperation and learning**. Innovation is hampered when specialties do not connect with each other. Seek new methods, services, and products by working with people from different departments, professional disciplines, and organizations.

3. **Strive to share information**. Teach others how to use the information you have. Work to make sure ideas and information are flowing ... downward, uP, and [side] - [ways].

4. **Help others be successful**. Be sensitive to their needs. Avoid a self-centered approach. Demonstrate your support through your actions.

5. **Have an open mind. Be willing to change your opinion and behavior**. If innovations are to result from collaborative effort, the participants must be willing to think and act in new ways.

    This means that people must <u>take action</u> to bring about change, not just talk about it.

    Remember Liebling's Law:

    **WITHOUT CHANGE,
    THERE IS NO CHANGE.**

    People need to be open to new ideas, new methods, and new people. Thinking *"this is the way it's always been done"* is terribly limiting.

6. **Understand your team members.** Work at communicating your messages so that your intentions are understood.

7.   **Accept the challenge of continuously improving your organization**. Start by acknowledging that your organization (A) has problems, (B) can be much more effective, and (C) has untapped potential.

Then, encourage **everyone** to accept the challenge of working together to reduce the problems and to make continuous improvements.

The key is to make sure **everyone** understands it is good to put problems on the table and to talk about them. This leads to problem-solving and creative solutions.

Things to talk about:

- Installing new methods for achieving the organization mission.

- Improving/increasing teamwork.

- How to improve the process of work.

- The impact of organizational change.

- Opening up, and keeping open, communication channels between departments and levels.

- Changing out-dated policies and procedures.

- Reducing stress and inefficiencies between offices, headquarters, regions and field.

- Improving internal services or products that do not satisfy users.

- How to improve customer satisfaction.

TEAMWORK

WORK DONE BY SEVERAL ASSOCIATES WITH EACH DOING A PART BUT ALL SUBORDINATING PERSONAL PROMINENCE TO THE EFFICIENCY OF THE WHOLE.

By permission. From Webster's Ninth New Collegiate Dictionary © 1988 by Merriam-Webster Inc., publisher of the Merriam-Webster® dictionaries.

8. **Organizational development.** If your organization is going through a major change, it is really saying to itself:

How we currently do things is no longer useful to our purpose and is ultimately self-defeating.

We must do things differently.

2

For the organization to successfully shift from *where it is* to *where it needs to be,* employees, at all levels, need to think and perform in new ways. It is not business as usual.

If your organization is going through a change, the following list may be helpful in understanding what is needed.

You may need:

- To increase the number of people who network across traditional department lines and levels.

- To demonstrate respect, courtesy, and appreciation for each other.

- To invite new people to participate in meetings, and to create the environment so that these people feel good about participating.

- To decrease the amount of complaining, and to have fewer put-downs and criticisms when you have very little first-hand information.

- To place new names on distribution lists for reports and memos.

- To meet each other's needs more.

- To have more of the following:

  Good idea.

  Let's try it.

  We can.

  Let's get more information and give it a chance.

Team Opportunity Exercises

27. **Team improvements at work.** What THINGS TO DO suggestions do you feel are needed in your workplace?

28. **What can you do to improve your workplace?** Which THINGS TO DO suggestions can you support? What do you feel you can put into action that will improve your workplace?

29. **Team improvements at home.** What THINGS TO DO suggestions can you apply in your family life?

2

TEAM QUESTIONS

1. As good as we are, what can we do to be even better?

2. What do you need from me that will help you be more productive?

3. What do you need from me that will help you reach your goals?

4. Does our team's mental attitude support our team goals?

TEAM-ESTEEM

Team-esteem (team pride) is how the team feels about itself. Teams with high team-esteem rely on each other and feel that they can accomplish almost anything. They affirm themselves with positive self-talk.

TEAM ESTEEM AFFIRMATIONS

We encourage each other.

We look for ways to help each other.

We respect different viewpoints.

We continuously strive to improve ourselves and to add new skills.

We are creative in finding solutions when working through disagreements.

We share our knowledge so that each person can be more successful.

*We recognize that our future success
is a result of what we do today,
not on what we did in the past.*

*We take nothing for granted
when implementing our plans.*

We look forward to new challenges.

*We ask for input about our performance
from our team members and customers.*

*We believe in continuous improvement
and our actions reflect this belief.*

*We are actively in charge of our
behavior and we direct ourselves
toward our mission.*

We learn from our mistakes.

*We bounce back quickly
from any set-backs.*

We don't waste time fixing the blame.

*We eliminate outdated policies,
procedures, and methods.*

Team Opportunity Exercises

30. **Team affirmations**. Which Team-Esteem Affirmations do you feel your team needs to use?

31. **Team achievement**. Do you think your team limits itself by the way that it thinks? If yes, what do you think needs to change?

32. **Team-esteem**. Working with the people on your team make a list of the things you like about your team.

33. **Team confidence builder**. Working with the people on your team, list the successes, however large or small, that have been achieved during the past month, quarter or year.

34. **Get feedback to find out if your behavior supports teamwork**. Schedule time to listen to your team members (upwards, sideways, downward) about their perception of your behavior.

TEAM COMMUNICATION

Instructions: Place a checkmark next to the statement if you feel team improvement is necessary.

_____ Being a good listener.

_____ Inviting other people's points of view.

_____ Understanding new ideas.

_____ Agreeing to work things out when there is a disagreement.

_____ Asking for feedback and questions.

_____ Concentrating on what is being said.

_____ Being considerate of those who do not quickly understand the intended message.

IMPROVING TEAM MEETINGS

Instructions: Place a checkmark next to the statement if it applies to your meetings.

_____ Follow-up is weak.
_____ Too many.
_____ Too few.
_____ Pre-meeting agendas are used.
_____ Everyone participates.
_____ Purpose of meeting is clear.
_____ The right people are there.
_____ Start on time.
_____ Scheduled in advanced.
_____ Too many unscheduled.
_____ Late arrivals.
_____ There is a leader or facilitator.
_____ Unprepared attendees.
_____ Visuals are used.
_____ Pre-meeting reading materials
        are distributed beforehand.
_____ Non-urgent matters are
        allowed to interfere.
_____ Irrelevant discussions occur.
_____ Written minutes are
        produced promptly.

2

TEAM GOAL SETTING

People who work together need to be involved in setting goals that affect them.

EXAMPLES OF TEAM GOALS

- Quality
- Customer Satisfaction/Service
- Quantity
- Interpersonal relationships
- Financial
- Development of new products/services
- Development/application of technology
- Human resource development
- Research
- Organizational efficiency

Team Opportunity Exercise

35. **Team goal setting**. As a team, select a work goal you want to work on. Then, proceed through the 7-step Plan of Action (p. 28 - 31).

TEAM PRODUCTIVITY

People who work together need to communicate with each other about activities in their organization which they feel waste time or do not make sense. This builds the "continuous improvement" culture.

2

TALK TO EACH OTHER

- *Look, this problem is recurring, it occurs over and over and over again. Let's invest our time so that we can prevent this problem from happening again. We'll all win.*

- *Are there things that I do that you feel wastes your time or causes you inefficiency?*

- *Let's get this out in the open so that we can work together to create some practical solutions.*

TEAM BRAINSTORMING

The purpose of brainstorming is to involve people in producing ideas that relate to a specific problem or objective. Write these ideas on an easel for everyone to see. The more ideas the better.

One person speaks at a time. Building on each other's ideas can be very productive.

All views are valid. No criticism and judgments like *It won't work.*

Emphasize creativity and "new thinking." Be unconventional.

For example, when looking at a process of work, think of unbundling the parts and then bringing the parts together in new, imaginative ways.

Save decision-making until all ideas have been presented. Then, discuss and put ideas in categories and priority order.

TEAM PROBLEM-SOLVING

Problem-solving is an important skill and process. So that everyone can be involved, consider breaking into smaller teams and then sharing the ideas from each team.

OUTLINE

2

1. Acknowledge a problem exists.

2. Define the problem. Ask why.

3. Make a commitment.

4. Gather data.

5. Identify possible options for solving the problem.

6. Evaluate these options.

7. Choose what to do.

8. Implement your plan.

9. Observe the results.

THINGS TO DO

1. **Acknowledge that a problem exists**. The very first step is to recognize that a problem exists.

2. **Define the problem. Ask why**. Get to the root cause(s) of the problem. Make sure you know the difference between the "symptom" and the "cause."

   Do not make the mistake of jumping to a solution before you have carefully analyzed the situation. Allocate sufficient time for this step.

   Ask lots of questions and do not accept superficial answers. Ask "why" over and over again. Obtain different points of view concerning the cause(s) of the problem.

3. **Make a commitment**. Don't go any further unless you are determined to implement one of the options.

4. **Gather information**. The amount of information you need depends on the complexity of the problem. Be objective. Do not rely solely on numbers. Listen to the people who are involved; find out why they think and feel the way they do about the situation. Dig for information. Be thorough. Double check your sources.

2

5. **Identify possible options for solving the problem**. This is the time to produce ideas and specific proposals. Remember: Being practical may only produce temporary benefits, not a long-lasting solution.

6. **Evaluate possible options**. Critically and objectively analyze your options. If time permits, test several of your options for real-world analysis. What are the good points, and bad points, for each option you are considering? What are the long-term and short-term considerations?

Get clear on what you want to accomplish.

Ask yourself:

> *How does the proposed solution(s)
> relate to ... organization mission, people
> affected, customer satisfaction, quality,
> return on investment, timeliness, and
> technology?*
>
> *Is there a hidden opportunity here?*

7. **Choose what to do**. Select the best
    option among those considered.

8. **Implement your plan**. This is the
    real-world step where you take action
    and follow-up on your plan. It requires
    determination to succeed, persistence,
    patience, and teamwork.

9. **Observe the results**. As you are
    implementing your solution, watch to see
    if it is working as you expected. Are
    modifications necessary? Do you see
    any unintended consequences, good or
    bad?

QUALITY
CUSTOMER
SERVICE

QUALITY
CUSTOMER SERVICE

The purpose of our work is to provide a service or product that satisfies customers. Satisfied customers (clients) build your reputation, making it that much easier to get new ones. LISTENING to, LEARNING about, and BEING RESPONSIVE to customers are the personal qualities you need so that you can satisfy your customers.

There are two types of customers, external and internal.

*Some employees have direct contact with "**external**" customers (clients). These people are outside of your organization.*

*Other employees serve "**internal**" customers (clients). These are people in other departments, plus people in your own department.*

Many employees have direct contact with both kinds of customers (clients).

THINGS TO DO

1. **Say "thank you."** Thank your customers (clients) for their business and the opportunity to serve them.

2. **Customer's perspective.** Try to understand the services and products you provide from the point of view of your customers and clients. Remember: Customers and clients are PEOPLE, with feelings, needs, and expectations.

3. **Make it easy for your customers to do business with you and your organization.**

   Good questions to ask your customers are:

   Are there things you feel we should improve on?

   How can I (we) make your experience with us more positive?

4. **Listen to and learn all you can about your customers (clients)**. Meet with them face-to-face or on the telephone. Ask lots of questions and listen carefully. Remember: Although you may not get many complaints, things may not be okay.

    Assess customer needs and requirements on a continuing basis. This will then allow you to adapt your policies and procedures to meet their (changing) needs.

    Good questions to ask are:

    Do you anticipate any upcoming changes that we can (I can) help you with or prepare for?

    How else may we serve you?

5. **Share information with others in your organization**. Share the customer information you gather and your ideas with other people in your organization.

Remember: Teamwork and collaboration are absolutely necessary to provide consistent customer satisfaction.

6. **Welcome complaints; they are an opportunity**. To you the problem may be small, but to your customer, the problem is special and important.

   Complaints are valuable in three ways.

   They provide opportunity to:

   - Help a person in need.

   - Fix a problem in the organization.

   - Stimulate ideas that can lead to new services, new products, and improved operations.

   Remember: You can build customer loyalty by handling complaints willingly and effectively. (See page 88-89)

Challenge Yourself Exercises

36. **Which quality customer service THINGS TO DO suggestions will you use more frequently?**

37. **List the services and/or products that you produce.**

38. **Who is your customer?** Who uses your services or products? List the people or departments that use your services or products.

39. **Why do your customers use your services or products?** Find out what your service or product enables your customer to accomplish.

40. **Measuring customer satisfaction.** Do you have a method that measures or indicates how well your customers are satisfied?

CUSTOMER SERVICE CREED

A CORPORATION MAY SPREAD ITSELF OVER THE ENTIRE WORLD AND MAY EMPLOY A HUNDRED THOUSAND PEOPLE, BUT THE AVERAGE PERSON WILL USUALLY FORM HIS OR HER JUDGMENT OF IT THROUGH CONTACT WITH ONE INDIVIDUAL.

IF THIS PERSON IS RUDE, UNCARING, OR INEFFICIENT, IT WILL TAKE A LOT OF KINDNESS AND EFFICIENCY TO OVERCOME THE BAD IMPRESSION.

3

EVERY MEMBER OF AN ORGANIZATION, WHO, IN ANY CAPACITY, COMES IN CONTACT WITH THE PUBLIC IS, IN A SENSE, A SALESPERSON.

THE IMPRESSION HE OR SHE MAKES IS AN ADVERTISEMENT, GOOD OR BAD.

DO YOUR BEST TO MAKE POSITIVE IMPRESSIONS. STRIVE TO BUILD POSITIVE RELATIONSHIPS WITH PEOPLE.

HANDLING
CUSTOMER PROBLEMS*

1. Listen. Show concern.

2. Ask questions to get facts.

3. Find out what the customer wants.

4. Determine a course of action.

5. Tell the customer what you intend to do.

6. Initiate steps so that the action is implemented within a stated time frame.

7. Follow-up. Make sure the action was implemented and the customer was satisfied. Directly communicate with the customer, when possible.

8. Share information so that others in the organization learn of the situation and can make improvements.

---

* You may want to customize this outline to fit your own needs.

Challenge Yourself Exercises

41. **How can you apply the Handling Customer Problems outline in your work?**

42. **Customize to fit your needs**. Do you think that any steps in the Handling Customer Problems outline have been left out? If so, what would you add?

43. **Prevent problems**. Think of an external customer or internal customer problem that you regularly encounter.

   - Why do you think the problem occurs in the first place?

   - What do you think can be done to prevent the problem from happening again?

   - Who needs to be included to implement the solution?

TELEPHONE SKILLS*

1. **Make it easy for the caller to do business with you**. <u>Remember</u>: Every caller needs assistance.

2. **Pay attention** to:
   - Caller's NAME
   - Stated PURPOSE of call
   - FEELINGS of the caller

3. **Call-backs and referrals**. Always get:
   - Name
   - Number (include area code)
   - Purpose of the call

4. **Helping phrases**: How can I help you?

   What can I do for you?

   Let me have your name and number and I'll see to it that (___name___) gets your message.

---

* Contributed by Nancy Friedman/The Telephone "Doctor"®/St. Louis, MO.

TELEPHONE SERVICE

Quality telephone service helps to keep customers and to get new ones.

THINGS TO DO

1. **Prompt answering**. Make sure the telephone is answered within three rings. (Example of performance standard: 95% of incoming calls are answered within three rings.)

2. **Easy does it with "On Hold."** In-coming callers should never be left hannnnngging "on hold." Few things are more irritating to a caller.

3. **Have a "willing to help" attitude**. Build relationships with callers by coming across as friendly, pleasant, and willing to help. For example:

   Thanks for calling, please feel free to call again.

   Is there any way I can help you?

4. **Make it easy for people to reach you**.
   When you are away from your telephone,
   establish a procedure that lets your
   customers know how to reach you or
   when you will return. <u>Remember</u>:
   Prompt access to you may be a critical
   factor for your customer's success, as
   well as your own.

5. **Careful with call forwarding**. When you
   use call forwarding, double-check to
   make sure the phone at the other end is
   being answered, and answered
   appropriately.

6. **Answering machines**. Messages left on
   your machine need to be responded to
   promptly.

7. **Quality check**. Have temporary
   employees serve on the telephone only
   after they can demonstrate a level of
   service that meets your satisfaction.
   Your business image can be damaged by
   a well-intentioned person who does not
   correctly use the phone, or does not
   have basic information to share with
   callers.

Challenge Yourself Exercises

44. **Which telephone service THINGS TO DO suggestions will you use?**

45. **Check your voice quality**. If you are not sure how your voice sounds or how fast or slow you speak, tape record your voice. Then review the tape for possible self-improvement.

46. **"Willing to help" attitude**. What phrases do you use that make your callers feel you are friendly and willing to help?

3

47. **Quality check**. Call your department or your own phone number (when it is on call forwarding). How is it working?

ACHIEVING QUALITY CUSTOMER SATISFACTION

Instructions: Place a checkmark next to the statement if you feel it applies to your organization.

_____ Procedures are too rigid.

_____ Procedures are too loose.

_____ Standards of performance not clear.

_____ Not enough teamwork within my department.

_____ Not enough teamwork between departments.

_____ We have good ideas, but we don't implement them very well.

_____ We make too many errors.

_____ Follow-up with customers is weak.

_____ We don't get the information we need.

HEALTH
ACHIEVEMENT

HEALTH ACHIEVEMENT*

*A person with high self-esteem is usually
healthy and less stressed. Use stress for
growth by facing life with enthusiasm. Think
of life as a challenge to grow, not as a
problem. Focus clearly on what it is you
want.*

THINGS TO DO

1. **Self-Esteem**. Accept who you are and
    choose to grow. Love yourself.
    <u>Remember</u>: You are what you think, so
    continually say to yourself.

    I can.   I will.   I am.

    Read and think about the thoughts on
    pages 10 - 12, 14 - 16, and 103 at least
    twice daily. Do this for three weeks so
    that you develop the habit of thinking this
    way.

---

* This chapter contributed by John P. Kelly, M.D.,
Pittsford, N.Y. Dr. Kelly is a practicing physician who
specializes in Internal Medicine and Sports Medicine.
A "Toastmaster of the Year" award-winner, Dr. Kelly
speaks on Health Achievement.

2. **Self-motivation. Choosing.**
   Enthusiasm comes from directing your
   motivation from your own <u>internal</u>
   controls. Stress comes from directing
   your motivation from <u>external</u> controls.

Internal Controls	**External Controls**
I want to.	*I have to ...* *because if I don't* *do it, I pay a* *terrible price.*
I choose to.	

3. **Positive attitude toward change**. When
   change enters your life, choose a
   positive attitude; this will result in growth.
   Maintain persistence, patience, and
   self-esteem. Continually repeat to
   yourself (self-talk):

   I can.   I can.   I can.

4

4. **Wheel of Life - Balance**. Your <u>Wheel of Life</u> turns readily when your goals are in balance. Choose your goals so they are clear and distinct.

   Allocate appropriate time in all areas.

- **Mental** ● **Physical** ● **Spiritual**

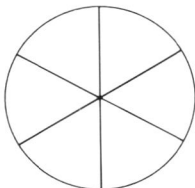

- **Social** ● **Financial** ● **Family**

Balance	Lack of Balance
Aliveness	Dis-ease
Joy	Stress

5. **Communicate with your care-giver**. Be
    prepared to provide your significant
    medical history to your care-giver.
    Always be truthful and provide the full
    picture.

    Explain to your care-giver any significant
    changes in your lifestyle (deaths, new
    job, job layoff, money problems ....).
    Express your fears and worries to your
    doctor.

6. **Exercise Prescription (minimum).***
    Your overall aim is to achieve and
    maintain ideal weight and physical
    condition.

    In general, exercise three times weekly,
    on non-consecutive days, for thirty
    minutes each time.

    4

    Exercise to a level where you can talk
    easily, but not sing. (This corresponds
    well to various formulas for pulse rates
    and age.)

  * **Important: Check with your care-giver
     for his or her exercise prescription**.

7. **Learn and use relaxation exercises**.
    Here are some that may help you.

Deep Breathing Exercise

Lie on your back or sit in a chair with
your hands at your side in a comfortable
position. Close your eyes. Now, inhale
deeply and hold your breath for a count
of three. Then, exhale slowly, breathing
out as much of the air as possible. As
you exhale, try to visualize the tension
leaving your body.

Do this deep breathing exercise at least
six times and try to stay in this relaxing
position for at least ten minutes.

If you are aware of tension in a particular
part of your body, such as your shoulder
blades, tell it to let go of its tensions: *My
shoulder blades are relaxing and the
tension is leaving my body.*

Mental Visualization

While sitting or lying in a comfortable position, visualize in your mind a place that has been relaxing for you. Include as many of your senses as possible:

I am at the beach, lying on the warm sand, with the warmth of the sun shining on me. I smell the salt air and hear the waves gently breaking. In the distance I see seagulls gliding in the air.

Warm Bath

Take a warm bath for ten minutes. Try to enjoy the sensuality of the warm water on your body. Place a warm washcloth on your face and enjoy its heat.

4

Foot Massage

Massage your feet (top, sole, toes, heel, sides). This is easy to do and it feels wonderful.

Reading or Hobby Break

Get absorbed in something that is not related to the activity that is causing you stress.

Challenge Yourself Exercises

48. Which health achievement THINGS TO DO suggestions and relaxation exercises will you use?

HEALTH AFFIRMATIONS

*I enjoy a great sense of well-being
after regular exercise.*

*I choose my friends and associates
carefully for their positive attitudes.*

*I learn from my past
and create my future.*

*I recognize that my mental health
reflects my good physical fitness.*

*No matter what infirmity or limitation I may
have, there is always appropriate exercise
for me to maintain good conditioning.*

4

*I minimize my stresses
by regularly exercising.*

*I choose to set aside time
for meditation and spiritual growth.*

*I cheerfully accept myself as I am and
purposefully attempt to correct my faults.*

WEIGHT-LOSS AFFIRMATIONS

*I carefully choose the foods I eat
for their taste, flavor, and nutritional value
and remain aware of good weight control.*

*I choose to be one of the 150 million
Americans who are at or near ideal weight.*

*I choose to eat all foods
in appropriate quantities.*

*As I attain and maintain my ideal weight,
my sense of well-being and confidence
increases.*

*I regularly direct my self-conscious mind
to visualize and achieve my ideal weight.*

*When I eat properly
I am energetic, active, and alert.*

Note: If you choose to participate in a weight-loss program, it is important to: (1) Affirm your desire to lose weight and to reach your ideal weight. (2) Exercise to help get the weight off. (3) Exercise to tone muscles and help get rid of fat.

WORKSHOPS
AND
SEMINARS

5

WORKSHOPS AND SEMINARS

Attending a workshop, seminar, or class is an investment in your continuous improvement and skill development.

To get the most value from your workshops and seminars, **there are things you can do before, during, and after** *your learning experience.*

THINGS TO DO - Before

1. **Goals**. Clarify in your mind what it is that you intend to get from the seminar, workshop, or class. This is your goal. Write this down and refer to it. (You may have more than one!)

2. **Motivation**. Understand your motivation for attending. Expect wonderful things to happen.

3. **Preparation**. Read something about the subjects beforehand. Complete any pre-meeting assignments.

THINGS TO DO - During

1. **Mental approach or attitude**.
   Participate in learning experiences with the attitude:

   I want to learn all I can.

   I will find what I am looking for.

   I am open to new experiences.

   Minimize distractions, like phone calls from your office.

   If you find yourself thinking more about things to do at work than about the seminar, try this: List on a sheet of paper what you are thinking about; then try to mentally set aside these thoughts, knowing you can refer to the list later on.

2. **Try to find personal relevance to the material**. Think about how you can use the information and the experience to achieve goals and to make improvements.

5

3. **Listen carefully and participate**.
    Ask questions. Express your feelings
    and share any "Aha" experiences with
    other participants. If there are exercises,
    actively participate.

4. **Notes**. Take notes of key points and
    new ideas.

5. **Experiment with new behavior**. Your
    workshop or seminar may be an
    excellent place to try out new behavior.
    For example:

    (A) If you are usually a follower, act
    more like a leader.   (B) If you are a
    leader, follow someone else's leadership.
    (C) If you are typically quiet and
    reserved, be more verbal.   (D) If your
    notes usually fill hundreds of pages, take
    only a few notes and be involved in new
    ways.   (E)   If you usually sit in the back
    of the room, sit in front.
    (F) If your attitude is "Prove it to me" or
    "It won't work" try a different approach:
    "What good things could happen if this
    did work?"

THINGS TO DO - After

1. **Use what you learn. Follow-up. Take action**. If you did not write your goals or an action plan during the seminar, write one within a few days.

   Use your appointments calendar to schedule follow-up time. This is time when you review your notes, study the material, and work on specific items.

2. **Goals and motivation**. Identify what you want to improve and achieve. These are your goals.

   Keep your motivation (your reasons for wanting or choosing your goal) fresh in your mind. Remember:

   I can. I can. I can.

   We can. We can. We can.

3. **Support teams**. Inform your co-workers and bosses about the seminar. If appropriate, ask for their specific support.

5

4. **Personal letter**. Write a letter to yourself about your workshop experience. Include:

    - what was new
    - what was a review
    - what new ideas were triggered in your mind
    - how you felt
    - what skills you want to use
    - what improvements you want to make

    Re-read and refer to this letter for reinforcement.

    For extra reinforcement, make copies of what you write. Then, arrange for a copy to be mailed to you at 30-, 60-, and 90-day intervals.

Challenge Yourself Exercises

49. **Which workshop and seminar THINGS TO DO suggestions do you think you will use more frequently?**

APPENDIX

SALES ACHIEVEMENT CHART

Activities	Daily	Weekly	Monthly
SELF-IMPROVEMENT Worked on building self-esteem, managing time, clarifying your plan of action, visualization skills.	minutes	minutes	minutes
VISUALIZATION—REHEARSING Studied benefits and features of your services and products.	minutes	minutes	minutes
Practiced your sales presentation.	minutes	minutes	minutes
Practiced questions that will uncover customer needs.	minutes	minutes	minutes
LEADS Telephone calls made.	number	number	number
SALES PRESENTATIONS	number	number	number

SALES AFFIRMATIONS

My number one priority is the client.

I am alert to anyone and opportunities to sell _____.

Closing sales and satisfying customers are the most important aspects of my job.

I have tremendous product knowledge and it's easy for me to communicate the benefits with individuals and organizations when I discuss _____ with them.

It's easy to ask questions and get the information I need.

I am well-planned and professional.

My income is growing and I am now netting $ _____ per month.

Clients buy from me because I help them solve problems.

LIFE PLANNING

Developing a personal philosophy of life and a plan will provide you direction and meaning.

Your life plan describes what you are hoping your life will stand for. Your plan will help you organize and take charge of your life so that you move it in the direction that matters to you.

THINGS TO DO

1. **Develop a personal philosophy of life**. What do you hope your life will stand for?

2. **Believe that you have choices**. Obtain information that will allow you to see more options for how you want your life to unfold.

3. **Identify your strengths**. Ask other people for their opinion of your strengths; too often, we do not see our many qualities.

4. **Identify any significant frustration**. If the frustration has been continuous, work to resolve it, do not let it linger.

5. **Do not let negative thinking or unreasonable fears limit your vision**. Do not remind yourself over and over again of past mistakes, errors or missed opportunities in your life. Do not blame others for your life situation. Do not give other people the power to control what you do and how you feel. Do not judge your life against the lives of others.

6. **Take responsibility for choosing and achieving your life plan**. Do things daily that move you closer to your goals.

    Use the Life Planning Chart on page 116 as a model to help you visualize your life plan.

    Refer to the Setting Goals and Plan of Action sections in this handbook.

LIFE PLANNING CHART

AREA OF YOUR LIFE*	Now	10 years from now	20 years from now	30 years from now	__ years from now
	Year:	Year:	Year:	Year:	Year:
	Your age:	Your age:	Your age:	Your age:	Your age:
	*	*	*	*	*
	*	*	*	*	.*
	*	*	*	*	*
	*	*	*	*	*
	*	*	*	.	*
	*	*	*	*	*
	*	*	*	*	*
	*	*	*	*	*

*Filling in the details is like writing a movie script for your life.
*Refer to p. 20.

Challenge Yourself Exercises

50. **Which life planning THINGS TO DO suggestions will you use?**

51. **Set priorities**. Refer to Exercise No. 8. Why did you list and rank these areas of your life as you did? How might you rank them in 10 years? 20 years? 30 years?

52. **Your ideal day.** Describe a really terrific day, or week.

53. **What do you want your life to stand for?** If you could overhear a eulogy at your own funeral, what would you like to hear?

54. **What really matters to you?** If you had just one year to live, how would you like to live it? If someone you loved had just three months to live, how would you treat that person?

Challenge Yourself Exercises

55. **What are the qualities you like most about yourself?** (See Exercise No. 2) What might you do with your life to better express these qualities?

56. **What can you do to make your life work better for you?**

PRE-RETIREMENT PLANNING

Planning and researching your options before you retire can help ensure that your retirement years will be enriching and satisfying.

THINGS TO DO

1. **Preparation**. Begin planning and collecting information at least five to ten years before the time when you think you will retire. You can start financial planning in your thirties. If retirement time is close, start immediately.

2. **Develop a vision for your future**. You want a mental outlook that focuses on the future. Think about "retiring to" something in the future, not "retiring from" something in the past.

3. **Develop goals that are meaningful for you**. What are the things that matter? If you have a spouse, encourage your spouse to develop goals.

   Develop a balance between your personal goals and your spouse's goals.

4. **Stay organized**. Purchase a folder or notebook with pockets so that you have a place to keep track of your ideas and the written materials (brochures, articles) you will likely collect.

5. **Be resourceful**. Make sure the information you collect is up-to-date; otherwise you may be making decisions based on faulty assumptions. You can find materials and resource people at libraries, government agencies, banks and insurance companies.

   Talk to people who have retired and sift through what they tell you. Be careful about "old tales" that may not be up-to-date. Read newspapers from other cities to stimulate ideas. Obtain professional assistance if needed.

6. **Time management**. Collecting information and sharing ideas with your spouse requires time. Investing one hour per week on pre-retirement planning produces over 50 hours of yearly preparation.

7. **Volunteering**. Volunteering before you retire is a great way to learn about upcoming opportunities for your retirement years. When you volunteer, you will discover whether or not you like certain activities.

Challenge Yourself Exercises

57. **Which pre-retirement planning THINGS TO DO suggestions will you start with?**

58. **Motivation**. List ten reasons why you are, or will be, looking forward to retirement.

59. **What are you good at and what is appealing to you?** List everything you have ever done that was fun, interesting, or personally fulfilling.

60. **Do you have a secret dream?** Write down the things that interest you, but you have not yet tried.

61. **Where would you like to live?** Do you think you will stay where you are or will relocate? What is right for you? Look at: housing, climate, health care, transportation, proximity to loved ones and friends, recreation, arts, and cost of living.

REARING CHILDREN

The following <u>Twenty Memos From Your Child</u> were seen on a wall plaque in a gift store. Author unknown.

1. Don't spoil me. I know quite well I ought not to have all I ask for. I am only testing you.

2. Don't be afraid to be firm with me. I prefer it; it makes me feel more secure.

3. Don't let me form bad habits. I have to rely on you to detect them in the early stages.

4. Don't make me feel smaller than I am. It only makes me behave stupidly "big."

5. Don't correct me in front of people if you can help it. I'll take much more notice if you talk quietly in private.

6. Don't protect me from consequences. I need to learn the painful way sometimes.

7. Don't make me feel my mistakes are sins.

8. Don't be upset when I say "I hate you." It isn't you I hate, but your power to thwart me.

9. Don't nag. If you do, I shall have to protect myself by appearing deaf.

10. Don't tax my honesty too much. I'm easily frightened into telling lies.

11. Don't make rash promises. Remember that I feel badly let down when promises are broken.

12. Don't forget that I cannot explain myself as well as I should like. This is why I am not always very accurate.

13. Don't be inconsistent. It completely confuses me and makes me lose my faith in you.

14. Don't push (put) me off when I ask questions.

If you do, you will find that I stop asking
and seek my information elsewhere.

15. Don't tell me my fears are silly. They are
    terribly real and you can do much to
    reassure me, if you try.

16. Don't ever think it is beneath your dignity
    to apologize to me. An honest apology
    makes me surprisingly warm towards
    you.

17. Don't ever suggest that you are perfect
    or infallible. It gives me too great a
    shock when I discover that you are
    neither.

18. Don't forget I love experimenting. I
    couldn't get on without it, so please put
    up with it.

19. Don't forget how quickly I am growing
    up. It must be very difficult for you to
    keep pace with me, but please try.

20. Don't forget that I can't thrive without
    lots of understanding love.

CONTINUOUS
IMPROVEMENT

To improve myself, I need to do the following:

_____

_____

_____

_____

_____

_____

_____

_____

_____

_____

NOTES

QUANTITY ORDERS

Handbook for PERSONAL PRODUCTIVITY (Revised Edition) is available at special discounts for bulk purchase use:

- organization-wide
- sales promotion
- premium
- fund-raising
- educational

Please contact:

Productivity Press
P.O. Box 13390
Portland, OR   97213-0390
Telephone: (503) 235-0600
Telefax: (503) 235-0909
E-mail: service@ppress.com